W9-BEH-994

We Make Soup!

By Leslie A. Rotsky

Scott Foresman
is an imprint of

PEARSON

Glenview, Illinois • Boston, Massachusetts • Chandler, Arizona •
Upper Saddle River, New Jersey

Photographs

Every effort has been made to secure permission and provide appropriate credit for photographic material. The publisher deeply regrets any omission and pledges to correct errors called to its attention in subsequent editions.

Unless otherwise acknowledged, all photographs are the property of Pearson Education, Inc.

Photo locators denoted as follows: Top (T), Center (C), Bottom (B), Left (L), Right (R), Background (Bkgd)

Opener: ©B. Blue/Getty Images; **1** ©Shubroto Chattopadhyay/Corbis/Jupiter Images; **3** Photos to Go/Photolibrary; **4** ©Will Heap/©DK Images; **5** ©Michel Touraine/Jupiter Images; **6** ©Randy Faris/Corbis/Jupiter Images; **7** ©Shubroto Chattopadhyay/Corbis/Jupiter Images; **8** ©B. Blue/Getty Images.

ISBN 13: 978-0-328-46340-4
ISBN 10:   0-328-46340-X

Copyright © by Pearson Education, Inc., or its affiliates. All rights reserved. Printed in the United States of America. This publication is protected by copyright, and permission should be obtained from the publisher prior to any prohibited reproduction, storage in a retrieval system, or transmission in any form or by any means, electronic, mechanical, photocopying, recording, or likewise. For information regarding permissions, write to Pearson Curriculum Rights & Permissions, One Lake Street, Upper Saddle River, New Jersey 07458.

Pearson® is a trademark, in the U.S. and/or in other countries, of Pearson plc or its affiliates.
Scott Foresman® is a trademark, in the U.S. and/or in other countries, of Pearson Education, Inc., or its affiliates.

8 9 10 V010 14 13

I have the carrots.

I have the potatoes.

I have the beans.

I have the tomatoes.

I have the onions.

Mom has the spoons!